IT'S TIME TO EAT CHOCOLATE ICING

It's Time to Eat CHOCOLATE ICING

Walter the Educator

Silent King Books
A WhichHead Entertainment Imprint

Copyright © 2024 by Walter the Educator

All rights reserved. No part of this book may be reproduced in any manner whatsoever without written per- mission except in the case of brief quotations embodied in critical articles and reviews.

First Printing, 2024

Disclaimer

This book is a literary work; the story is not about specific persons, locations, situations, and/or circumstances unless mentioned in a historical context. Any resemblance to real persons, locations, situations, and/or circumstances is coincidental. This book is for entertainment and informational purposes only. The author and publisher offer this information without warranties expressed or implied. No matter the grounds, neither the author nor the publisher will be accountable for any losses, injuries, or other damages caused by the reader's use of this book. The use of this book acknowledges an understanding and acceptance of this disclaimer.

It's Time to Eat CHOCOLATE ICING is a collectible early learning book by Walter the Educator suitable for all ages belonging to Walter the Educator's Time to Eat Book Series. Collect more books at WaltertheEducator.com

USE THE EXTRA SPACE TO TAKE NOTES AND DOCUMENT YOUR MEMORIES

CHOCOLATE ICING

It's time to eat, oh, what a sight,

It's Time to Eat
Chocolate Icing

Chocolate icing, pure delight!

So creamy, smooth, and full of cheer,

The sweetest treat is finally here!

It sits on cakes, it tops a bun,

It's sticky, gooey, lots of fun.

A little taste, a tiny lick,

Chocolate icing does the trick!

With sprinkles bright or plain and sweet,

It makes a snack feel so complete.

On cupcakes small or brownies wide,

Chocolate icing is the pride!

It melts so soft, it shines so bright,

Like chocolate dreams in every bite.

A finger scoop, just one, okay?

It's hard to stop; it's yum all day!

It's Time to Eat Chocolate Icing

We spread it round, we spread it high,

On cookies tall, it loves to lie.

A swirl, a dollop, oh, so grand,

Chocolate icing by your hand.

It's made for fun, for tasty play,

It turns a treat from dull to yay!

A little dab, a little spread,

Chocolate icing paints food red!

But wait, not red, that's just a tease,

It's chocolate brown, made just to please.

On waffles, muffins, pies so sweet,

Chocolate icing can't be beat.

Is it dessert or snack or more?

It's everything we all adore.

A secret bite, a happy face,

It's Time to Eat Chocolate Icing

Chocolate icing takes first place!

Now let's all share, no need to fight,

A spoonful here, a spoonful right.

Chocolate icing's fun to share,

A treat that shows how much we care.

So grab a spoon, it's time to go,

For chocolate icing steals the show.

A tasty treat, a messy bliss,

It's Time to Eat
Chocolate Icing

Who could resist a treat like this?

ABOUT THE CREATOR

Walter the Educator is one of the pseudonyms for Walter Anderson. Formally educated in Chemistry, Business, and Education, he is an educator, an author, a diverse entrepreneur, and he is the son of a disabled war veteran. "Walter the Educator" shares his time between educating and creating. He holds interests and owns several creative projects that entertain, enlighten, enhance, and educate, hoping to inspire and motivate you. Follow, find new works, and stay up to date with Walter the Educator™

at WaltertheEducator.com

www.ingramcontent.com/pod-product-compliance
Lightning Source LLC
LaVergne TN
LVHW052011060526
838201LV00059B/3968